MATH ATTACK!
Exploring Life Science with Math

EXPLORING KILLER PLANTS WITH MATH

Robyn Hardyman

PowerKiDS press.
New York

Published in 2017 by
The Rosen Publishing Group, Inc.
29 East 21st Street, New York, NY 10010

Cataloging-in-Publication Data
Names: Hardyman, Robyn.
Title: Exploring Killer Plants with Math / Robyn Hardyman.
Description: New York : PowerKids Press, 2017. | Series: Math attack: exploring life science with math | Includes index.
Identifiers: ISBN 9781499431292 (pbk.) | ISBN 9781499431315 (library bound) | ISBN 9781499431308 (6 pack)
Subjects: LCSH: Carnivorous plants--Juvenile literature. | Dangerous plants--Juvenile literature.
Classification: LCC QK917.H349 2017 | DDC 583'.75--dc23

Produced for Rosen by Calcium
Editors for Calcium: Sarah Eason and Jennifer Sanderson
Designers for Calcium: Paul Myerscough and Jennie Child
Picture researcher: Rachel Blount

Picture credits: Cover: Shutterstock: Cozyta tl, Kuttelvaserova Stuchelova br; Inside: Shutterstock: 13Smile 12, Bluerain 18, 29t, Caner Cakir 16, Cyrustr 21, Dimijana 9, F_studio 26, Martin Fowler 5, 28t, Jeep2499 8, Iakov Kalinin 20, Dasha Kolesnikova 14, 28b, Lone Wolf Photography 4, Dariusz Majgier 11, Steve Mann 24, Maridav 15, Mikeledray 19, AleksandarMilutinovic 10, Nastya Pirieva 17, Lance Sagar 13, Brandon Seidel 23, Sinephot 22, Andrea J Smith 27, SusaZoom 1, Tarbell Studio Photo 25, 29b, Marco Uliana 6, Egon Zitter 6–7t.

Manufactured in the United States of America
CPSIA Compliance Information: Batch #BW17PK: For Further Information contact Rosen Publishing, New York, New York at 1-800-237-9932.

CONTENTS

STAYING ALIVE

Plants are everywhere. Experts are still not sure exactly how many **species** of plants there are in the world, but their best **estimate** is about 422,000. Plants may look beautiful, but some are very harmful. They can sting or be poisonous enough to kill.

The angel trumpet vine grows in the forests of South America. Its flowers are beautiful, but they contain a substance that can **hypnotize** people.

No Getting Away

Unlike animals, plants cannot run away from **predators** that want to eat them. They cannot hide, either. They have few of the tricks that animals use to stay alive. Animals that eat only plants are called herbivores, and there are many of them. To get enough food, herbivores need to eat a lot of plants every day, so the plants are under attack. However, plants do have some ways of protecting themselves. Some have spines and thorns to wound animals that come too close. Their most powerful weapon, however, is **poison**.

Poison!

A poison is a chemical that causes harm to an animal if it gets inside the animal's body. Some poisons can even cause harm just by coming into contact with an animal's skin. Substances that are poisonous, or **toxic**, are called **toxins**. Plants can poison the animals that eat their leaves, flowers, and seeds, or that touch their stings and spines.

gympie-gympie

MORE THAN A NUMBER!

AUSTRALIA'S GYMPIE-GYMPIE TREE IS THE WORLD'S MOST TOXIC TREE. IT IS ALSO THE MOST PAINFUL OF ALL STINGING PLANTS. THE TERRIBLE BURNING SENSATION IT CAUSES WHEN IT TOUCHES THE SKIN CAN LAST FOR UP TO 2 YEARS.

Spurge laurel is quite common in public parks, but it is highly poisonous. Eating just a couple of its berries can make an animal's or a person's **internal organs** bleed and fail, causing death.

MEAT EATERS

Plants make their own food. They take the energy in sunlight and turn it into food using a process called **photosynthesis**. For some plants, however, this is not enough. They eat meat to add to their diet. Anything that eats meat is called a carnivore, and these carnivorous plants are bug killers.

Snap!

Probably the best-known carnivorous plant is the Venus flytrap. It has a pair of thick, padded leaves covered with hairs. When a bug lands on a leaf and touches the hairs, the leaves snap shut. Spikes along the tops of the leaves are like prison bars, trapping the bug. The plant then releases chemicals to break down the bug's body into a liquid that it can digest.

Carnivorous plants like the Venus flytrap often grow in poor-quality soils, so they need the extra food they get from bugs.

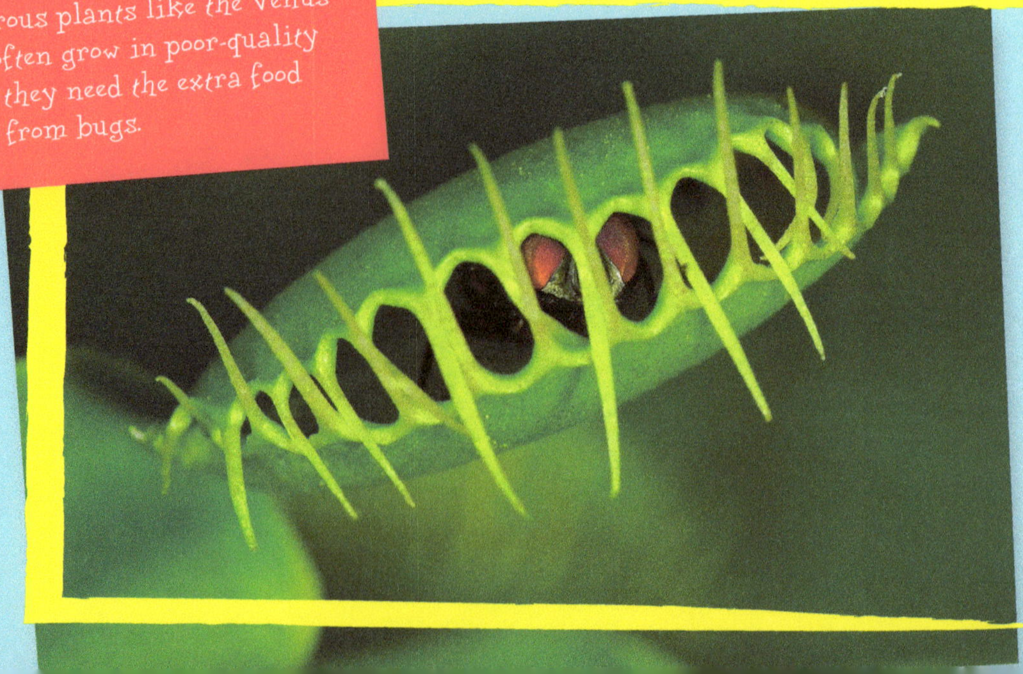

Insects are attracted to pitcher plants by their bright colors and the scent they give off.

Attractive Scent

Other carnivorous plants attract their prey by giving off a scent that insects like. Pitcher plants are shaped like tall vessels. They contain a sweet-smelling **nectar** that attracts insects. The inner walls of the pitcher are slippery, so when an insect lands on the pitcher, it slides down inside and is trapped. It drowns in a pool of liquid at the bottom and its body is broken down to be digested.

MATH ATTACK!

Sundew plants are another type of carnivorous plant found in many habitats. One type of sundew from Australia has spoon-shaped leaves that each have up to 18 snap-tentacles. When an insect touches the sundew, its snap-tentacles toss the insect to the center of the leaf, where it is digested. The snap-tentacles can move four times faster than the blink of an eye. If a sundew has 6 leaves, how many snap-tentacles can it have in total? Use this calculation to help you solve the problem:

6 LEAVES X 18 SNAP-TENTACLES PER LEAF = ? SNAP-TENTACLES TOTAL

CASTOR

The most poisonous plant in the world, according to the *Guinness Book of World Records,* is the castor plant. This is definitely one to keep well away from!

The castor plant is attractive, so it is popular with gardeners.

Truly Nasty

Castor plants grow naturally in the Mediterranean area, east Africa, and India, but because they are pretty, people grow them in many other locations as well. They have attractive, pointed leaves and bunches of furry-looking seeds. It is these seeds that are so deadly. They contain a poison called ricin. Just one seed contains enough poison to kill a person in two days. It is a painful, horrible death. Castor seeds are large, and are called beans when they dry out.

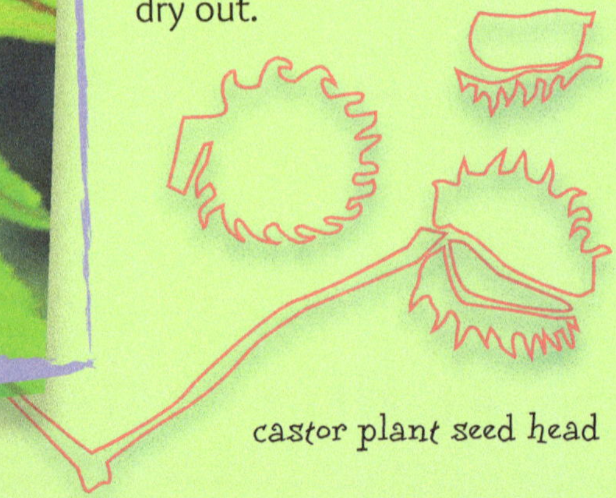

castor plant seed head

Castor beans contain the deadly poison ricin. It is powerful enough to kill humans and other animals.

MORE THAN A NUMBER!

SOME ANIMALS' BODIES RESPOND MORE STRONGLY TO THE POISON FROM CASTOR BEANS THAN OTHERS DO. HUMANS RESPOND ESPECIALLY BADLY TO RICIN. WE WOULD NEED TO CONSUME 1 OR 2 BEANS TO KILL US, BUT IT TAKES 11 BEANS TO KILL A DOG, AND AS MANY AS 80 TO KILL A DUCK.

Helpful Seeds

Strangely, castor beans can also be helpful. When they are pressed, they produce a yellow oil, called castor oil. This is not at all poisonous, and for centuries, people have found many uses for it. Today, some people drink a little of it to help their digestion. It is also used in cosmetics and soaps, and is a source of **biodiesel**, an alternative kind of fuel used in the diesel engines of motor vehicles instead of gasoline.

MUSHROOMS

Mushrooms are a kind of **fungi**. They do not need sunlight to make their food. Instead, they break down organic matter, such as leaves, to get their food. Many of them are poisonous, so to stay safe, you should never pick any mushrooms in the wild.

Not a Fairy Tale

The fly agaric mushroom looks just like the mushrooms in picture books. It has a bright red cap covered in white spots. However, this plant isn't from a fairy tale. It's poisonous enough to kill cats and dogs, and it can make people very sick. The jack-o'-lantern mushroom is found widely across the United States. It is so named because it glows in the dark; but do not be tempted to pick one of these beauties either, as they are highly toxic.

Jack-o'-lantern mushrooms look attractive, but never be tempted to touch or eat them.

Deadliest of All

There is one stand-out mushroom to avoid, and that is the death cap. It looks quite ordinary, but it has caused more human deaths than any other mushroom. It even killed the ancient Roman emperor Claudius. It causes severe damage to the liver and kidneys, and even just 1 ounce (30 g), which is about half a mushroom, is enough to kill an adult. Often, poisonous mushrooms become less toxic when they are cooked, but not this one!

Death cap mushrooms often grow as just a single mushroom alone.

MATH ATTACK!

There are about 6,000–7,000 cases of mushroom poisoning in the United States every year. There are about 30 species that can kill people, and 20 more that can make people very sick. They include the deadly-sounding destroying angel mushroom, the panther cap, and the autumn skullcap. How many species of poisonous mushrooms are there in the United States? Use this calculation to help you solve the problem:

30 DEADLY + 20 HARMFUL = ? SPECIES OF MUSHROOMS

GIANT HOGWEED

Can you imagine a plant that will harm you severely if you simply touch it? Surely no plant could be that toxic? Well, this one is. The giant hogweed grows widely in the northeastern United States and in Europe, often along canals and riverbanks.

The spotted stem of giant hogweed can help you identify it.

Do Not Touch!

The giant hogweed is, as its name suggests, huge. It can grow much taller than an adult person. Its stem is stained with reddish-purple spots, and has fine spines. The danger lies in its sap. This is a sticky liquid inside the leaves and stems that oozes out when you touch it. On the skin, the sap reacts with sunlight and causes severe burns and swelling. These effects can last for many months, or even years. If the sap gets in your eye, you could go blind.

Fast Spreader

Giant hogweed is an **invasive** species. This means that it spreads rapidly, invading a place where it doesn't belong. A single giant hogweed plant produces tens of thousands of seeds every year. These are spread by birds and along waterways, and take over new areas.

MORE THAN A NUMBER!

THE GIANT HOGWEED CAN GROW UP TO 20 FEET (6 M) TALL. IT HAS LEAVES UP TO 5 FEET (1.5 M) WIDE AND PRETTY WHITE FLOWERS IN AN UMBRELLA SHAPE. THESE CAN ALSO BE 5 FEET (1.5 M) WIDE EACH. THE PLANT LOOKS SIMILAR TO ITS HARMLESS RELATIVE, COW PARSNIP, WHICH IS SMALLER.

If a person finds giant hogweed growing, they should call in professionals to cut it down.

Water Hemlock

Watch out because water hemlock is the most poisonous plant in North America. It is found almost anywhere where there is water, such as along rivers, lakes, shores, swamps, and marshes.

Do not be tempted by the lacy prettiness of water hemlock: its poison is deadly.

Look-Alikes

This plant looks like a smaller version of giant hogweed, but the plants are not closely related. It also looks like cow parsnip, which is harmless. It stands up to 8 feet (2.5 m) tall and its white flowers are made of clusters of tiny flowers. All its parts are poisonous: leaves, stem, flowers, and roots. Eating just a small amount will cause seizures, or fits, as well as vomiting and stomach cramps. People have died just a few hours after eating this plant. In ancient times, the poison hemlock was used as a punishment. A famous **philosopher** in ancient Greece, named Socrates, was was forced to eat hemlock and died.

People who live in the wilderness or visit nature reserves must know which plants are safe to use.

Life in the Wilderness

Many people like to learn about how to survive in the wilderness. They discover how to find food, build shelters, and enjoy the wildness of nature. It is important, however, to know which plants to avoid when you are out **foraging**. The stems of water hemlock are hollow, so people enjoying wilderness survival trips have been tempted to use them as drinking straws. You can imagine this has had very unpleasant, and even deadly, results.

MATH ATTACK!

Along the banks of a river, water hemlock plants are growing. In every 50 yards (46 m) there are 20 hemlock plants. How many plants are there in a stretch of riverbank 250 yards (230 m) long? Use this calculation to help you solve the problem:

250 YARDS ÷ 50 YARDS = ? SECTIONS

20 PLANTS X ? SECTIONS = ? PLANTS

Rosary Pea

Some killer plants have poison in every part, for maximum effect. Others concentrate their deadly power in their seeds. The rosary pea is one of those plants. It is a common climbing plant in **tropical** areas. You do not even have to eat rosary pea seeds to suffer their deadly effects. They are so toxic that they can kill a person who is just handling them.

Rosary pea seeds look attractive clustered inside their seed pods.

Deadly Seeds

The rosary pea is also known as crab's eye or jumbie bead. It twines up around trees and shrubs. Although the plant is harmless, its seeds are most definitely not. They are also really pretty (bright red with a black dot), which is why they have traditionally been used for making jewelry and for other decorative purposes. Inside the seeds, however, is a deadly poison called abrin. This is similar to the ricin found in castor plant seeds (see pages 8–9), but it is about 75 times more powerful.

Jewelry is often made of seeds and beans. Avoid any made with rosary pea seeds.

Dangerous Work

In parts of the world where people use rosary pea seeds for crafts, it can be very dangerous work.
To string together the dried seeds or beans, people need to drill small holes in them. People have died just from pricking their fingers on the sharp points used to drill those holes.

MORE THAN A NUMBER!

IF A PERSON SWALLOWS ROSARY PEA SEEDS WHOLE, THEY ARE LESS LIKELY TO BE KILLED THAN IF THEY CHEW THEM. THE OUTER CASING OF THE SEEDS GIVES SOME PROTECTION FROM THE POISON INSIDE. HOWEVER, A DOSE OF THE POISON AS SMALL AS 2 GRAINS OF SUGAR IS ENOUGH TO KILL A PERSON.

In Your Backyard

Some toxic plants are rare and grow in remote places far from most people. There are others, though, that can be found in surprising locations. You might think you would be safe from deadly plants in your own backyard, but think again. Some common garden plants are extremely poisonous, so be sure never to put the parts of any garden plant in your mouth. They can give you a headache or a stomach ache, cause fits, or worse, even kill you.

Foxgloves grow in many pretty colors, but all are harmful if you eat them.

Ordinary Hazards

Foxgloves make lovely spires of colorful flowers in a garden border. The plant's other names, such as rabbit flower and witches' thimbles, give a clue to how pretty it is. Bees love to go right inside the flowers to reach the nectar. Although they look attractive, foxgloves contain a powerful substance that does serious damage to the heart if it is eaten. The leaves of the plant do, too. Another flowerbed heart-stopper is aconite, also called wolfsbane or monkshood. Its poison is so powerful that eating just 0.7 fluid ounce (20 ml) can kill a person within hours.

So Pretty

The lovely, cascading purple flowers of climbing wisteria are poisonous, and so are bushy hydrangeas. Those little white lily-of-the-valley that arrive in early spring, and are so fragrant, will also make you very sick if you eat any part of them. The safest way to enjoy a garden is with your eyes only.

wisteria

The stems of rhubarb are good to eat, but the leaves are poisonous.

MATH ATTACK!

The vegetable patch is home to some pretty scary plants, too. Did you know that the leaves of potatoes, rhubarb, and chili peppers are all poisonous to eat? Imagine a potato plant has 75 leaves. The leaves drop off as the growing season advances. The plant loses 5 leaves every day. How many days will it take for the plant to lose all of its leaves? Use this calculation to help you solve the problem:

75 LEAVES ÷ 5 = ? DAYS

PUBLIC HAZARDS

Public spaces are great places for running around and enjoying the delights of fragrant and flowering plants. Whether you are out in a meadow, in a park, or a backyard, plants are all around. Beware, though: some plants that grow in public spaces are deadly.

Lovely Buttercups?

Buttercups, for example, are a common sight in fields and meadows. Their bright yellow flowers light up the landscape. Yet they contain a toxin that can give us a rash if we touch them. Worse, if we happened to eat a lot of them, we could die. It is important to keep grazing animals away from buttercup fields, as they become sick when they eat them, too.

Buttercups make a lovely display in summer, but do not be tempted to touch them.

Make sure you know if any oleander plants are in your schoolyard or backyard.

Park Disasters

Parks and backyards are often planted with flowering shrubs. Some of these should be avoided. The colorful flowers of azalea and rhododendron bushes look pretty, but the leaves and flowers make your mouth burn before you start vomiting and your heart slows down. The most dangerous shrub is the oleander. Oleander is planted for decoration, sometimes in schoolyards. It looks beautiful, but every part of it contains a toxin that can give you a heart attack if you eat it. Breathing in the smoke from a burning oleander can be harmful.

MORE THAN A NUMBER!

YEW TREES ARE **EVERGREEN**. THEY CAN GROW UP TO 90 FEET (27 M) TALL OVER HUNDREDS OF YEARS, WITH A TRUNK UP TO 6 FEET (1.8 M) WIDE. THE SMALL LEAVES ARE VERY TOXIC AND SO ARE THE SEEDS. THESE NESTLE INSIDE THE RED BERRIES, WHICH ARE NOT ACTUALLY POISONOUS THEMSELVES.

SEA DANGERS

Most of the dangers in the sea come in the form of animals that hunt other animals. Think of deadly sharks, with all those terrible teeth. Most of the plants in the sea are harmless seaweeds, but in some places, and at certain times of year, sea plants can be deadly.

Red Tide

Along coastlines at certain times of year, the sea appears to turn a rusty red, as if it has turned to blood. This is not blood, however, it is a sea of **algae**. Algae are very tiny seaweeds, and when thousands of them join together, they form a huge carpet over the surface of the water, and up the beach. This often happens when the temperature changes suddenly, and when certain **nutrients** that feed the algae appear in the water. This scary event is called a red tide and it happens almost every summer along the Gulf Coast of Florida.

The red tide looks like a sea of blood crashing onto the shore.

A Poisonous Meal

These algae are highly toxic. Fish and shellfish are poisoned when they eat them, and when birds eat the fish, they are poisoned, too. Whole beaches have been covered with the bodies of dead fish and birds in a red tide. Unfortunately, this poison is also very harmful to us. If we eat shellfish that have eaten the algae, we can lose feeling in our arms and legs, and have difficulty breathing.

A red tide can kill large numbers of fish and birds along the shore.

MATH ATTACK!

Red tide blooms can last for days, weeks, or months. Imagine a red tide begins along the coast of Florida on June 1, and lasts until June 29. The following year, it begins on June 10 and lasts until June 17. How much shorter is the second red tide than the first? Remember that you need to count both the first day and the last day. Use this calculation to help you solve the problem:

1 TO 29 = ? DAYS = A

10 TO 17 = ? DAYS = B

A – B = ? DAYS SHORTER

STINGS AND SPINES

Some plants have defenses other than poison. They deliver stings that make us leap away or have sharp spikes and spines that hurt whoever touches them. Some stingers are even killers.

The tiny hairs on stinging nettles give a painful sting when we touch them.

Stingers

Stinging nettle leaves are covered with tiny hairs that deliver stinging chemicals to our skin when we touch them. It is uncomfortable for a few minutes, but not dangerous. The New Zealand nettle tree, however, is a different story. This gruesome tree can kill a person who happens to brush against it. It is a monster version of a stinging nettle, growing up to 15 feet (5 m) tall. Everything about it is supersized. Its huge leaves have bigger hairs that deliver a stronger poison that can kill an adult. If a person survives it, and that is not certain, they will be in pain for months.

Stay Sharp

Some plants have sharp weapons, such as spines or thorns. In hot, dry places, cactus plants grow with fleshy stems and spines. These are better at holding onto water than leaves. Other plants, such as agaves and yuccas, are just too spiky to get close to. They are designed for defense, and are great at keeping away animals. Some trees can even protect themselves with spines, such as the honey locust tree. Its trunk is covered in sharp spines.

MORE THAN A NUMBER!

CACTUS PLANTS GROW IN DIFFERENT SHAPES AND SIZES. SOME ARE MORE THAN 32 FEET (10 M) TALL, OTHERS NO MORE THAN A FEW INCHES TALL. HONEY LOCUST TREES ARE MUCH BIGGER. THEY CAN REACH 65–98 FEET (20–30 M). THAT IS A LOT OF SPINES.

Cactus spines cover the whole plant, to keep predators away.

A World of Plants

The world of plants is full of amazing variety and beauty. We have flowers and shrubs in our gardens, majestic trees in our parks, and forests full of plants of every size and kind. Yet, while plants are part of what makes our world so beautiful, they can also be deadly.

You cannot tell from looking at it that white snakeroot is highly poisonous.

Built for Defense

Plants, like all living things, need to stay alive. Their deadly weapons are for defense, to keep them from being eaten. If a cow eats white snakeroot, for example, it becomes sick. It will be less likely to eat that plant again. Unfortunately, when people drink the milk of those sick cows, they get sick, too. People think this is what happened to the mother of President Abraham Lincoln. She died of "milk sickness" from cows that ate white snakeroot.

snakeroot

Skunk cabbage looks like an alien—and it's dangerous!

A Clear Message

Sometimes, the message to stay away is loud and clear. The skunk cabbage of the swamps of North America smells so bad that humans and animals don't want to go near it. It looks like an alien, it stinks, and is poisonous to eat, too. Other plants have spines and thorns as warning signs. Some plants are sneaky killers and hide their poison behind a beautiful appearance. For that reason, it is best just to admire unfamiliar plants from a distance.

MATH ATTACK!

Imagine that a stinging nettle plant has 150 leaves. Each leaf has 200 stinging hairs on it. How many stinging hairs are there on the whole plant? Use this calculation to help you solve the problem:

150 LEAVES X 200 STINGING HAIRS = ? STINGING HAIRS

ANSWERS

Now that you have read about killer plants, try to learn more. It would be good to find out about the plants in your backyard or schoolyard. Here are the answers to the Math Attack problems. How did you score?

PAGE 7:

6 LEAVES X
18 SNAP-TENTACLES PER LEAD
= 108 SNAP-TENTACLES

PAGE 11:

30 DEADLY + 20 HARMFUL = 50 SPECIES OF MUSHROOMS

PAGE 15:

250 YARDS ÷ 50 YARDS
= 5 SECTIONS

20 PLANTS X 5 SECTIONS
= 100 PLANTS

PAGE 19:

75 LEAVES ÷ 5
= 15 DAYS

PAGE 23:

1 TO 29 = 29 DAYS = A

10 TO 17 = 8 DAYS = B

29 – 8 = 21 DAYS SHORTER

PAGE 27:

150 LEAVES X 200 STINGING HAIRS
= 30,000 STINGING HAIRS

GLOSSARY

algae Small seaweed plants.

biodiesel A diesel fuel made from plants or animal waste.

estimate To form a general idea about the value, size, or cost of something.

evergreen A plant that does not lose its leaves in winter.

foraging Searching for food.

fungi Living things that do not photosynthesize and include molds, mildews, mushrooms, and yeasts.

hypnotize To put a person into a trance so they are unaware of their actions even though they are awake.

internal organs A body part, such as the heart, that performs a specific function.

invasive Spreading rapidly.

nectar The sweet substance produced by flowers that attracts bees and other insects.

nutrients Substances that provide food energy.

philosopher A person who is a thinker and teacher.

photosynthesis The process plants use to make their food from the energy in sunlight.

poison A substance that is harmful.

predators Animals that hunt other animals for food.

sensation Feeling.

species A type of living thing.

toxic Poisonous.

toxins Poisons.

tropical In the areas of the world close to the equator, to the north and south.

FURTHER READING

Books

Claybourne, A. *Killer Plants and Other Green Gunk* (Disgusting and Dreadful Science). New York, NY: Crabtree Publishing, 2014.

Largo, M. *The Big Bad Book of Botany: The World's Most Fascinating Flora*. New York, NY: William Morrow, 2014.

Spilsbury, L. *Creeping Killers: Extreme Plants* (Extreme Biology). New York, NY: Gareth Stevens, 2015.

Stewart, A. *Wicked Plants: The Weed That Killed Lincoln's Mother and Other Botanical Atrocities.* Chapel Hill, NC: Algonquin Books, 2009.

Websites

Due to the changing nature of Internet links, PowerKids Press has developed an online list of websites related to the subject of this book. This site is updated regularly. Please use this link to access the list:

www.powerkidslinks.com/ma/killerplants

INDEX